How To Find Your Soulmate

The Humorous Women's Guide To Avoiding The Risks Of Online Dating Scams

(How To Find And Identify Your Soulmate Or Life Partner: The Ultimate Guide)

Elias Pfleger

TABLE OF CONTENT

Be Noticeable 1

Appreciate and value yourself, both internally and externally. 16

Anxiety and Lack of Confidence will Result in the Loss of the Relationship 50

Stop waiting; start becoming! 90

That Thing Called Confidence 115

Be Noticeable

If the individual for whom you hold sincere concern lacks sufficient knowledge about your person, it behooves you to undertake measures that would command their attention.

They lack sufficient acquaintance with your character to develop emotional attachment, potentially explaining their failure to experience romantic affection toward you. By distinguishing yourself, you will not only capture their attention, but also have the potential to alter their perspectives.

There are several strategies through which you can distinguish yourself in an appealing manner. You can assume the role of the focal point at the event, don unconventional and attention-grabbing attire, engage in unique and stimulating activities, or even simply initiate contact by introducing yourself.

While one's physical appearance may not solely determine their ability to inspire romantic feelings, it undeniably plays a significant role. Therefore, putting effort into presenting oneself in an appealing manner by dressing to impress is highly advantageous. Indeed, there is no inherent fault in appearing aesthetically pleasing.

The greater your level of attractiveness, the higher the likelihood that individuals, particularly those who are not acquainted with you, will be inclined towards you. Enhance your appearance significantly through a comprehensive transformation, commanding the attention and admiration of everyone as you gracefully move through the corridors.

CHAPTER III

Do something exciting

Acquiring the skill of directing one's focus inward and endeavoring to enhance oneself exemplifies a viable approach to cultivating attractiveness. Stepping outside of your comfort zone entails engaging in novel activities and embarking on daring adventures.

While it may pose a certain level of difficulty, it will assuredly amplify their focus and attentiveness towards you.

Individuals possessing qualities such as attractiveness, a penchant for adventure, an exhilarating demeanor, and a fervent disposition are decidedly more inclined to procure the companionship they desire. Instead of adhering to your usual routine, embracing spontaneity and embracing new adventures adds an intriguing quality to your persona. Reigniting the passion in a enduring romantic relationship is equally crucial due to this factor.

Strategies for Cultivating an Unconditionally Affectionate Partnership

Given our understanding of the characteristics representative of genuine love, what steps can we undertake personally to foster a more affectionate and compassionate relationship? In the first instance, it is crucial to acknowledge that notwithstanding these apparent differences between genuine love and illusion, numerous individuals erroneously conflate the two. They might even have a preference for imagination over reality, as it is more agreeable to be emotionally attached to someone rather than genuinely experiencing close intimacy with them.

Many individuals became engrossed in the enchanting narrative, the superficial aspects, or the outward manifestation of the relationship (i.e. its visual presentation as opposed to its emotional essence) (i.e its external appearance as opposed to its internal sensation). We might develop affection for the semblance of connection or assurance that the situation provides, but we refrain from forming an intimate bond with the individual involved. This is because, despite our professed desire for love, we often engage in behaviors that repel it. Hence, the initial stride towards cultivating a more affectionate nature is to acquire the knowledge and ability to scrutinize our inhibitors.

1. Questioning the obstacles that impede genuine love

Numerous individuals possess apprehensions regarding proximity that they may not even be consciously aware of. While we may exhibit tolerance towards satisfying our yearnings for romantic encounters within the realm of literature, more often than not, we demonstrate an aversion towards attaining such desires in actuality. The experience of being cherished by another individual has the potential to disrupt our emotional boundaries, giving rise to dormant feelings of sorrow and fear that originated in early infancy. Both the act of giving and receiving love have a tendency to disrupt our negative, yet familiar, self-perceptions. On a subconscious level, it is possible that we harbor a belief that embracing love would disrupt the very fabric of our familiar universe and leave us questioning our personal identity.

Due to these factors, we often find that we are the primary obstacle when it comes to finding and maintaining a significant relationship. It is imperative that we acquaint ourselves with the defenses we possess that act as barriers against the embrace of love. For instance, in case we were raised experiencing rejection, we may harbor reservations about developing an intimate connection with another individual. We may harbor doubts regarding our ability to place genuine trust or reliance on a partner, consequently resulting in either an inclination to cling onto them or push them away, ultimately leading to the identical outcome of creating emotional distance.

If we were subject to ridicule or disdain during our formative years, it is plausible that we may encounter challenges in possessing self-assurance or acknowledging our own value within interpersonal connections. We may actively pursue companions who exhibit familiar patterns of belittling us, or we may struggle to wholeheartedly reciprocate our partner's expressions of affection toward us due to the discomfort they create by challenging our initial self-perception.

In the event of encountering intrusion during the formative years or having a father who exhibited emotional neediness, it is possible for individuals to develop a tendency to completely avoid engaging in relationships and assume an artificial sense of independence. Conversely, some individuals may subconsciously gravitate towards individuals who rely heavily on them to fulfill their desires and needs, extending beyond what is expected. Furthermore, it should be noted that both of these extremes can potentially result in relationships that are devoid of genuine emotional connection and intimacy.

Fortunately, we have the opportunity to initiate a transformation of these harmful relationship patterns by gaining a deeper comprehension of our own selves and our defensive mechanisms. What factors contribute to our selection of the relationships we engage in? What are the favorable and unfavorable characteristics that evoke our attraction? Do we engage in tactics that distort or influence our spouse's responses in order to conform to our own defensive mechanisms? What is the method for creating distance? What behaviors do we engage in that may appear to be self-protective, but ultimately result in distancing oneself from love?

2. Distinguishing oneself from past influences that are no longer advantageous in the current context.

The process commonly referred to as differentiation involves the method of testing long-standing, entrenched habits and barriers. This process consists of four sequential steps:

Distinguish oneself from the judgmental, punitive, and detrimental attitudes that were absorbed during upbringing.

Distinguish oneself from negative traits observed in one's parents that manifest in one's own character.

Question and evaluate the instinctive responses that once served to protect your younger self but are now no longer advantageous in the present situation.

Envisioning and adhering to your principles - what kind of person do you aspire to become?

By embracing these degrees of differentiation, we enable ourselves to transcend a state of excessive caution and pursue the aspirations that define our lives.

What are the signs that someone genuinely loves another person?

It is not unprecedented to find oneself in a state of doubt regarding the authenticity of one's experience of true love. In light of everything, one might possess remarkably intense sentiments of sympathy and reverence for their partner, yet it remains a challenge to ascertain whether these sensations truly meet the criteria to be labeled as genuine love. Fortunately, there are a total of eight crucial indicators that can assist you in evaluating whether the experience you have encountered is authentic love or merely an illusion.

If one is unsure about the authenticity of their emotions being attributed to pure love, it becomes imperative to examine these eight fundamental indicators.

1. You have a deep and genuine concern for this individual. A clear and definitive sign that one has encountered genuine love is when they possess an unwavering and unconditionally affectionate regard for their partner. To put it differently, irrespective of any adversities that may come your way, and in both prosperous and challenging times, you provide unwavering support and demonstrate a heartfelt concern for this individual. Unwavering love lies at

the heart of the essence and nature of authentic love.

2. You wholeheartedly embrace and acknowledge your partner. Yet another indication of profound affection is the ability to comprehend and esteem the essence of one's beloved, cherishing them for their true essence. You are not making an effort to alter, mend, or transfigure your partner. Instead, you wholeheartedly embrace, hold in high regard, and deeply appreciate your partner, acknowledging their flaws and imperfections.

3. You are free to engage in conversation on any topic. When one has truly encountered genuine love, it signifies the ability to engage in open and sincere discourse on any matter with said individual. Genuine love implies a level of sincerity in your commitment to your

spouse, where you hold nothing back in terms of your personal history and are able to completely expose yourself emotionally to your partner. You possess an enduring emotional and physical intimacy, fostering a more profound bond in your romantic relationship due to your mutual inclination and ability to exhibit unguardedness and vulnerability towards one another.

4. You present your authentic self when interacting with this person. Once you have encountered true love, you possess the capacity to be utterly candid with your partner. You are not engaged in any form of deceit by assuming a false identity, inventing interests or pastimes, or exhibiting behavior that does not align with your true self. Authenticity plays a pivotal role in cultivating a meaningful connection within a romantic relationship.

5. You respect each other. Experiencing profound affection also entails a significant level of esteem, benevolence, and empathy existing within the relationship with one's spouse. Individuals can express empathy towards each other, comprehend each other's perspectives, and effectively address conflicts and disagreements in a manner that fosters productivity and upholds each other's welfare.

6. You have comparable values. In order to truly encounter genuine love, it is imperative that one's principles and values align harmoniously with those of their marital partner. Although there may be disparities between individuals, such as their upbringing, religious upbringing, or even their passion for football, true love entails shared values when it comes to distinguishing between right and wrong. To put it succinctly, the foundation of genuine love involves the mutual possession of parallel principles.

7. Mutual interaction of happiness levels occurs. When contemplating the authenticity of your feelings, it is imperative to closely observe your genuine sentiments and emotions. Does the act of bringing forth joy in this individual serve to imbue you with happiness as well? Do the acts of surprising and favoring your spouse also elicit a sense of exhilaration within you? When both you and your spouse possess a mutual aspiration to provide each other with delight and contentment, it is gratifying to acknowledge that you are indeed manifesting genuine love.

8. You're a team. Upon the recognition of authentic love, it signifies an unwavering commitment, unwavering dedication, and unwavering devotion to one another. Through genuine affection, you and your partner collaborate harmoniously as a cohesive entity, mutually bolstering and enriching each

other's lives. In lieu of behaving in a self-centered or self-important fashion, your perspective is oriented towards the collective rather than the individual. Regarding romantic affection, your partner is genuinely regarded as your collaborator and ally.

Appreciate and value yourself, both internally and externally.

One must cultivate self-love before being capable of loving another individual. In order to discover your ideal partner, it is imperative to recognize the unique qualities and attributes you possess that would undoubtedly appeal to a compatible individual in the realm of romantic relationships. In this activity, we will delve into your areas of strength, captivating personality attributes, and valuable qualities that are deserving of emphasis when constructing your online dating profiles.

Consider Your External Qualities

Commence by creating a dual-column enumeration on your paper or document. Please denote each of these sections as "External Qualities" and "Internal Qualities."

Your external attributes encompass the observable physical characteristics and skills that are evident to others, ranging from your well-proportioned physique to your captivating and expressive facial features. Would you be so kind as to inform me if you possess an exquisite vocal talent? Have you been informed that your smile is enchanting? Have you received any accolades or recognition for your proficiency in the field of writing? Discover all the elements that you find appealing which occur in the external environment. Although it may be only one aspect, seize it and capitalize on the opportunity.

Consider Your Internal Qualities
Subsequently, compile a comprehensive inventory of all favorable attributes that you possess internally. These are the characteristics that exert influence or

serve as the origin of our outward characteristics.

Do you possess strong maternal instincts and the ability to provide excellent care for children? Do you maintain honesty, even when encountering a mistake? Do you possess an optimistic attitude? Has it been suggested by others that you possess a generous nature? What are the fundamental components that constitute your individuality? Document them in the subsequent column.

Presently, kindly identify and encircle a selection of three to five discernible external attributes, as well as three to five intrinsic qualities, which you believe best reflect your character. This will construct a comprehensive portrayal of your true identity. These attributes shall be employed subsequently in our week-long expedition, as we craft and build your online profile.

Day three: Refrain from reflecting on the past.

This exercise is designed to assist us in discerning the characteristics which you will not be susceptible to in the future. If you have not previously entered into a romantic partnership, contemplate what aspects you would unequivocally exclude from your existence. This exercise adopts the identical approach as the one utilized in Day 2. Construct a page or document divided into two columns, clearly designating one side as "External Qualities" and the other side as "Internal Qualities."

Now, let us take into account your former partners and the adverse characteristics they exhibited. You may encounter some elements that are common to both categories, however, continue performing this exercise until you have populated both columns with the traits that you strongly detested in your previous relationships or anticipate disliking in your prospective first partner.

On the first day, we examined the factors leading to the termination of your relationships and delved into the reprehensible actions perpetrated by your former partners. Reflect upon this exercise as an opportunity to enumerate unfavorable external and internal attributes that you aspire to steer clear of. As an illustration, in the event that you have encountered mistreatment in a previous relationship, it may be advisable to include "hostile" under the category of internal traits, while incorporating "physically abusive," "verbally abusive," and comparable characteristics under the external attributes list.

Day 4: Engaging with Mr. or Mrs. in a formal meeting. Right (or Right Now)

Once more, we shall engage in the repetitive task of reiterating the uncomplicated exercise which we have previously undertaken during Day 2 and 3, aimed at discerning all the characteristics we desire to exist within our subsequent romantic liaison. Please contemplate the physical attributes that you desire in your future romantic partner. Subsequently, take into account the internal attributes they ought to possess. Please craft a two-column page or document, appropriately designating each side as "External Qualities" and "Internal Qualities," and commence the activity at present.

After completing the task, I request that you carefully evaluate your lists with a sincere perspective: Determine which qualities hold the utmost significance, and identify those which are dispensable. You will be the sole recipient of this information, therefore your candid response will greatly prove advantageous to you.

During the first day, we examined the factors contributing to the lack of success in your relationships or in finding a compatible partner. Certain students may have discovered through Questions No. 3, 4 or 5 that they encountered feelings of ennui within their previous relationships, leading to conflicts or their deliberate disruption of said courtships. A proportion of these students perceive these relationships as likely lacking success due to a lack of shared commonalities or interests between both partners. The most prosperous relationships are those in which a couple possesses shared values and interests, while also incorporating diversity into the equation. These couples shall forever present a source of exhilaration and ceaseless exploration, as each individual uncovers novel aspects of their partner.

Additionally, on the first day, you may have expressed that you believed your age or another attribute hindered your ability to secure dates. A subset of students have come to the realization that their prior attempts to secure romantic partners were predicated upon a highly unrealistic or exceedingly constrained set of criteria. While it is understandable that one may find an attractive blonde with notable physical features, who possesses a desirable sports car, captivating, it is important to acknowledge that such a preference may restrict one's options within a vast and diverse pool of individuals. This is the reason why this exercise holds significant importance.

Kindly indicate three to five external attributes and three to five internal attributes that hold significant importance to you. This will comprise the profile of your ideal match.

Prioritize Happiness Over Misery

Endure that strike, my companion. The impact of criticism pales in comparison to the enduring anguish of a solitary existence marked by countless lost chances. The opinions and statements of others hold little significance or relevance. The crucial factor lies in the selection and duration of one's auditory intake. It is evident that one would not choose to remain in the company of an individual who engages in verbal abuse and attempts to exert excessive control over one's actions.

Applying the same reasoning, do not permit your mind to subject you to mistreatment or dissuade you from pursuing a prospective romantic partnership. Cease fabricating justifications and commence embracing the essence of existence! The most unfavorable outcome would be abstaining from making an effort altogether. The most unfortunate circumstance one could encounter is to abstain from making an effort and instead anticipate the arrival of an idealized individual, without extending an invitation.

You have endured the most severe criticisms imaginable and have triumphed. Presently, it is the opportune moment to devote your efforts towards cultivating your state of well-being and affluence. Let us commence with a notably more compassionate and considerate Chapter 2.

Chapter 2
Attraction is Attraction
The commencement of a novel alliance is inevitably rooted in the presence of an initial attraction. In the absence of being

able to capture one's attention or displaying minimal initiative in doing so, the possibility of cultivating a relationship becomes exceedingly remote. The subtle stirring of romantic affection is what ultimately transforms individuals who are friends or acquaintances into romantic partners.

A considerable number of females derive satisfaction from being approached by males and having them initiate interactions. In an era of cultural evolution, there is a growing trend toward women garnering the interest of men, thereby rendering it more widely accepted.

Nevertheless, irrespective of the party initiating the action, the principle of attraction remains constant. The attraction cycle commences when an individual initiates a series of highly targeted actions. Despite widespread misconception, women do not effortlessly captivate the attention of men solely due to their exotic charm.

Many women who are able to effectively capture the interest of men do so intentionally, albeit their behaviors may possess a certain degree of subtlety. The majority of men are inclined towards visual stimuli and seek out aesthetic appeal. Hence, women who desire male attention exercise caution in their choice of attire to appear visually appealing.

Look the Part
Certain women strive to garner attention through the utilization of provocative attire, such as low-cut tops or short skirts, whereas others concentrate on accentuating their facial features and cultivating an appealing sense of fashion. This principle stands as the foremost guideline in the realm of captivating the attention of men. It is imperative that you present yourself in the most presentable manner possible.

Regardless of any perceived imperfections, it is imperative that you strive to present yourself attractively to others and cultivate feelings of attractiveness within yourself. Refrain from presuming that every individual who encounters you is preoccupied with your perceived imperfections. Merely engaging in the battle against detrimental thoughts does not imply that every individual you encounter shares in those same contemplations.

Who knows? It is plausible that your crush may be thinking, "What an endearing individual!" It is essential to refrain from making presumptions about the thoughts and perspectives of others. This behavior treads a delicate boundary between diminished self-assurance and unchecked suspicion. Why not afford others an opportunity?

Therefore, one's physical appearance holds no significance or bearing on their worth as an individual. Exert utmost effort to enhance your appearance and maintain a presentable look when seeking potential suitors. The level of attention and recognition you receive from others will directly correspond to the amount of effort and conscientiousness you invest in your personal presentation. Ladies who endeavor to appear elegant will garner attention. Conversely, a woman who displays indifference and ventures into public with a disheveled or unattractive appearance will not garner the same level of attention.

Please bear in mind that the energy you project into the world will reciprocate accordingly. When you venture into society, do you conscientiously consider both your facial characteristics and overall presentation? Do you commonly exhibit signs of joy, both in general circumstances and when encountering unfamiliar individuals? Does your smile emanate authenticity, or does it lean towards the closed lip type, which typically implies a sense of mistrust or cynicism? Do you often display a warm disposition or manifest signs of stress when gazing upon individuals?

When men engage in discussions concerning "appearances," we are not exclusively focused on your physical form or the outward image enhanced by cosmetic products. We indeed take notice of the subtleties, such as the radiance of your smile, the glimmer in your eyes, and the emotions conveyed by your countenance.

Indeed, the stern countenance of a woman would likely suffice to intimidate the majority of men and compel them to retreat.

Subliminal Communication

Another aspect of "appearance" remains, and frequently, this is the catalyst for the initiation of mutual attraction. Men tend to react to occurrences—precise actions or indications displayed by women that indicate a potential level of interest. Even if your behavior exhibits utmost subtlety, it will undoubtedly capture the attention of a gentleman. Despite the potential lack of awareness on the part of an individual, it is quite plausible that they may indeed perceive your signal and give you due attention.

What are some of the commonly employed cues employed by women to capture the interest of men?

Graceful Composure: Women aspiring to appear appealing often maintain an assured posture, typically characterized by aligned shoulders, an elevated chest, and a gently elevated nose. If a woman displays a posture that exudes strong confidence, it is likely to attract the attention of a man.

Regarding Visual Engagement: Whether a female individual maintains prolonged direct eye contact with a male counterpart or merely briefly directs her gaze towards him, the significance remains indistinguishable. Men invariably pay attention when a woman establishes visual contact. The eyes of an individual serve as a means of conveying emotions, and the greater the complexity of a person, the more captivating their eyes seem to be. To captivate a gentleman's interest while maintaining subtlety, establish visual contact and present a warm smile. Maintain a consistently focused gaze, and gradually shift your gaze away once you are confident that you have captured his attention.

Nonverbal Expressions: It is worth noting that individuals exhibit instinctive nonverbal cues, indicating their interest towards someone, which occur involuntarily. It's true. Several frequently observed nonverbal cues exhibited by females encompass:
• Running her fingers through her hair • Brushing her fingers through her hair • Combing her fingers through her hair • Ruffling her hair with her fingers • Gently tucking strands of hair behind her ear

• Gently stroking the surface of the glass with her fingertips

Engaging in physical contact with a gentleman or playfully striking him

• Moistening or nibbling her lips

• Enlarged pupils

• Extending or moving limbs in a rotary motion

These are a selection of the gestures that men take notice of and interpret, even if they possess limited conscious understanding of their exact connotations. If one finds themselves unconsciously engaging in these gestures, it is advisable to adapt accordingly by appropriately responding with affirmative nonverbal cues such as maintaining eye contact, offering a smile, and emitting laughter when suitable or appropriate.

Certain women who exhibit inherent tension or anxiety may exhibit noticeably unsteady and hurried movements. If you find yourself engaging in such behavior, endeavor to deliberately decelerate both your tempo and physical gestures. Females who exhibit a deliberate pace exude an aura of self-assurance and mastery—attributes that men will perceive as intriguing. I wanted to inform you that women commonly find themselves drawn to similar attributes in men as well.

Chapter 2

Get over past hurts.

One of the most expedient methods to make an erroneous selection or mar a relationship with the appropriate individual is to permit past wounds to infiltrate new relationships, whether through repetitive involvement in power struggles or by regarding your exceptional new partner with doubt or suspicion. In order to accurately discern the true nature of your newfound relationships, it is essential to acquire the capability to effectively cope with emotional suffering or, if necessary, address instances of emotional mistreatment.

Similar to intentional decisions to let go and move forward, maintaining a grasp on the past can also be a conscious choice. One characteristic that serves to unite us as individuals is our collective ability to endure suffering. All individuals have encountered various forms of adversity, encompassing both physical and psychological distress. The way in which each individual copes with such distress is what distinguishes us from one another.

Gaining wisdom from past experiences while directing attention toward growth and advancement are two of the most effective approaches to overcoming emotional wounds. We risk being confined to distressing sensations and memories if we allow ourselves to fixate on what might have occurred."

The subsequent 12 recommendations can offer you guidance in the process of releasing if you are endeavoring to progress after a distressing occurrence but lack clarity on how to initiate.

1. To counteract the disturbing concepts, devise a compelling catchphrase.

Your progress can be determined by the way you address yourself, as it is within your purview to either make strides or continue with no substantial development. The practice of employing a repetitive phrase to redirect one's thoughts amidst emotional turmoil often proves instrumental in enhancing cognitive realignment.

Dr. Carla Manly, a licensed clinical psychologist, provides an illustrative instance. Instead of fixating on my disbelief regarding this unfortunate incident.

Make an effort to recite an inspirational statement such as, "I possess the fortunate opportunity to embark upon an alternative path in my journey—one that is exceptionally well-suited for my personal growth and fulfillment."

2. Establish physical separation
It is customary to encounter recommendations advocating the maintenance of a certain level of distance from individuals or situations that cause distress.

According to clinical psychologist Dr. Ramani Durvasula, the suggestion of creating distance, whether physical or psychological, between ourselves and the person or situation could potentially be beneficial in terms of letting go. This is because it allows us to minimize our thoughts, mental processing, and reminders associated with the subject in question.

3. Work on your own.
It is imperative to prioritize one's own needs. You are required to make a decision regarding addressing the emotional pain that you have

experienced. Realign your focus on the present whenever you contemplate an individual who has caused you harm. Subsequently, direct your focus towards something for which you express gratitude.

4. Practice being aware.
According to Lisa Olivera, a marriage and family therapist, adopting a present-focused mindset can mitigate the impact of our past and future on our lives.
According to her, as we cultivate the habit of being mindful, the grip of our wounds over us diminishes and we gain greater autonomy in choosing our responses to life's challenges.

5. Be kind to yourself.
It is imperative to cultivate kindness and compassion towards oneself when plagued by incessant self-criticism for struggling to release oneself from a challenging situation.

In accordance with the remarks made by Olivera, this involves adopting an approach whereby we extend the same kindness and empathy to ourselves as we would to a dear companion, while also avoiding the temptation to draw comparisons between our personal path and that of others.

Nonetheless, according to Olivera, it is possible for us to opt for treating ourselves with care and affection when such situations arise. Pain is inescapable, and its inevitability cannot be denied.

6. Allow the negative emotions to arise.
Many individuals, like yourself, find solace in avoiding the encounter of distressing emotions due to apprehension. Indeed, as per Durvasula's research, individuals often harbor an apprehension towards experiences such as loss, anger, disillusionment, or sadness.

Individuals often exhibit a inclination to suppress or avoid certain emotions, rather than fully experiencing them, potentially impeding the process of emotional release. Durvasula asserts, "These distressing emotions bear resemblance to riptides." She offers counsel to allow one's thoughts and creative energy to naturally emanate. Engaging in conflict with them can result in you being stranded. Professional mental health support may be necessary.

7. Acknowledge that the perpetrator may be unwilling to offer an apology.

The pace of the healing process will be impeded should you wait for the other party to offer an apology. It is imperative to prioritize your recuperation in situations where you experience pain or distress, which involves acknowledging that the individual responsible for your injury will not extend an apology.

8. Practice self-care

On numerous occasions, it appears as though our only affliction is enduring pain following an injury. As per Olivera's perspective, self-care can manifest itself in various ways such as establishing limits, rejecting certain demands, participating in activities that bring us joy and ease, and prioritizing our personal needs. It is through the integration of self-care into our daily routines that we attain a greater sense of empowerment. "Our pains do not appear quite as overwhelming when we find ourselves in that particular state," she continues.

9. Engage in the company of individuals who exude positivity.
This concise, yet efficacious counsel will assist you in navigating a considerable amount of distress.
According to Manly, it is imperative that we recognize the impossibility of navigating through life single-handedly, and it is equally unrealistic to anticipate overcoming our emotional injuries in isolation. Embracing the notion of leaning on our cherished relationships and seeking their support emerges as an exceptional strategy to alleviate feelings

of solitude and to consistently reinforce the optimistic elements of our existence.

10. Please feel free to engage in discussions regarding this matter with other individuals.
It is of utmost importance to grant yourself permission to openly address challenging emotions or circumstances that have caused you emotional harm.

Per Durvasula's analysis, individuals at times struggle to progress because they hold the belief that discussing it is off-limits. This could be attributed to a possible waning interest from their social circle or the individual's inclination to abstain from broaching the topic due to personal embarrassment or humiliation. She clarifies.

However, it is essential to openly communicate. Durvasula recommends finding a compassionate and understanding individual, such as a trusted friend or therapist, who can be relied upon to attentively listen and provide guidance in relation to this matter.

11. Allow yourself the grace of forgiveness.

It might be imperative for you to direct your attention towards forgiveness, as awaiting an apology from the other party could potentially hinder your progress in overcoming the situation.

Due to its capacity to facilitate the release of accumulated emotions such as resentment, guilt, shame, or grief, forgiveness is imperative to the process of recuperation.

12. Consult a professional

It could be advantageous for you to seek assistance from a trained professional if you are encountering difficulties in overcoming the impact of a traumatic event. Occasionally, implementing these recommendations independently can pose a challenge, necessitating the assistance of a skilled professional to guide you.

The lesson
You are required to make a deliberate decision to assume control of the situation in order to release yourself from prior grievances. Although it may necessitate a certain amount of time and exertion. Commend your humble accomplishments and exhibit self-kindness as you engage in honing your perspective.

Dating a Pastor

Clergy members not only uphold the moral values of the religious institution, but also serve as role models for the congregation. When you consent to enter into a romantic relationship with a pastor, you are essentially acknowledging your acceptance of their religious convictions and attitudes towards romance.

Sex before marriage

Fundamentally, it is expected that pastors practice abstinence until marriage, as this is an integral aspect of their lifestyle and belief system, which might diverge from your own. It does not necessarily imply that each and every pastor possesses identical notions. Occasionally, a scenario may arise wherein he desires to engage in sexual activity prior to marriage, whereas you maintain a stance that refrains from such conduct. That's reality.

Regardless of the approach you choose, it is imperative to ensure that you engage in a thorough discussion prior to mutually committing to enter into a romantic partnership. Engaging in this activity at an early stage can facilitate a mutual determination concerning the acceptability of physical intimacy. If you happen to be the individual intending to engage in a romantic relationship with a clergy member, you possess the advantage of initiating the conversation. Oftentimes, the clergy member themselves may opt to evade such discussions due to concerns surrounding potential rejection without affording you the opportunity to ascertain its feasibility. In actuality, the choice to postpone physical intimacy until marriage is a matter of personal discretion. There are individuals who harbour a sense of unease towards this decision and opt to depart prior to the commencement of any substantial proceedings.

Busy schedule

Being in a romantic relationship with a clergy member can present challenges. It is imperative to comprehend that he is a prominent public figure, and frequently individuals believe they possess the entitlement to approach him at any given moment. The role of a pastor entails a workload that deviates from the conventional eight-hour workday, with little to no set schedule for duties. A clergyman's responsibilities encompass various tasks such as managing administrative duties throughout the day, conducting bible study sessions in the evenings, organizing leadership retreats on weekends, and occasionally attending to unforeseen emergency situations wherein individuals seek solace, encouragement, and advice. Regardless of the manner in which you strategize, you will inevitably encounter these challenges on numerous occasions. Such is the purpose for which he has been summoned and thus must fulfill it.

Taking into account all of these factors, one might commence pondering how they can fit into an extant and arduous regimen as a clergy member, the potential strain it can impose on the interpersonal connection, and whether one can endure a marital union with an individual of such nature. However, regardless of the size of the assembly and his unwavering dedication to the practice of ministry, there exists within him an enduring void that can only be occupied by your presence. You are the sole individual capable of occupying that vacant position.

Accept the spotlight

Irrespective of personal preferences, individuals will be inclined to seek proximity with you due to your close association with the pastor. Certain individuals may seek your association to further their personal objectives and enhance their own self-image, while others aim to exert influence over the pastoral decision-making process. There are numerous aspects of interest to you, yet you may encounter limitations that prevent their pursuit. This is attributable to the absence of privacy and close examination. If you are an individual who prefers to maintain a low profile, it is essential that you relinquish that inclination, for you are engaged in a romantic involvement with an individual whose occupation centers around public exposure. Having the role of a pastor entails being regarded as a public figure and, consequently, a source of inspiration. This implies that your personal life, irrespective of the efforts to keep it private, is essentially lived out before your church members and the broader community.

Church roles

This is important. If both individuals are members of the same church, it is advisable to minimize complications by restricting their involvement in church activities to the tasks they were engaged in prior to the commencement of their relationship. In the event that you have transitioned to his church subsequent to getting married, exercise caution in assuming immediate responsibilities. Indeed, you have become the esteemed confidant of the pastor, yet it is advised to proceed with caution, refraining from hastening the process and assuming the responsibilities befitting that of a matronly figure within the congregation. Allow such a role to unfold organically and in due course. As the partner of a clergy member, it is not inherently incumbent upon you to assume additional responsibilities within the church community. In a formal tone, one could rephrase the statement as follows: "Demonstrate an authentic portrayal of your character while devoting oneself to the service of the Lord."

Anxiety and Lack of Confidence will Result in the Loss of the Relationship

After arriving home, it is now opportune to reflect upon the current state of affairs. You encountered an individual towards whom you harbored an inclination, thereby arranging a subsequent gathering. Subsequently, he attended the rendezvous and a compelling dialogue ensued, further solidifying the positive nature of the encounter. In essence, it is evident that you hold a significant place in his thoughts at present. It is quite evident that he possesses some level of interest in you, as he would not have assented to your request of contacting him this week otherwise. Throughout both of those meetings, you effectively presented yourself in a favorable light by demonstrating respect towards the individual in question as well as towards your own self. This is the juncture at which we elevate our efforts to a more advanced level. Please consider sending him a text message tomorrow to inform him that you thoroughly enjoyed your time at the coffee shop. While it is true that you previously mentioned a timeframe of a few days for communicating this information, I would respectfully suggest considering a slight variation at this point. An alternate method of communication would involve sending a text message expressing that you recently came across a television advertisement promoting the forthcoming Padres game, which subsequently triggered reminiscences of the recipient. The text will serve as a gentle reminder, indicating to him that you are contemplating his presence.

Typically, this is the juncture at which numerous young women fail to retain the interest of their male counterpart. Indeed, I epitomize the exemplification of failure in establishing a romantic connection with a gentleman even prior to embarking on a consequential rendezvous. I have performed this task on numerous occasions, and my past encounters have instilled in me the importance of exercising utmost caution throughout the upcoming days. Failing to do so would not simply result in conveying an erroneous impression, but also result in the deterioration of the relationship. I vividly recall the overwhelming sense of enthusiasm I experienced following our brief encounter, as I hastily departed and eagerly sent him a message upon my arrival home. Subsequently, upon his lack of immediate response, I proceeded to send him an additional message. Subsequently, during the evening hours, I would diligently seek justifications to initiate communication with him via text messages. I would embellish my messages with delightful imagery of hearts and romantic couples enjoying their time on the seashore. I would convey to him the advantages and desirability of arranging a meeting during the forthcoming weekend. My infatuation with him was so overwhelming that I would metaphorically immerse him in my emotions.

Despite the current unfavorable appearance, the situation deteriorates further. I can recall departing from the coffee establishment and sending him a text message while in transit. I would politely inquire whether he deemed my attire aesthetically pleasing. I would inquire of him whether or not he admired my hairstyle. I would express to him that I found his scent quite pleasant and that it was challenging to refrain from physical contact. Indeed, this occurred subsequent to the aforementioned second gathering. In retrospect, it is understandable that these individuals chose to distance themselves from me. This recurring vulnerability I experience has consistently resulted in negative repercussions. I am aware that you have engaged in similar unwise actions. You may be actively engaged in performing those actions at this very moment as you peruse this text. Should you extract just a single lesson from this book, let it be the understanding that harboring personal insecurities will prove ineffective in garnering male interest. There exists a specific moment and context in which it would be appropriate to communicate with him in such a manner, rather than doing so when you possess very limited familiarity with him. I was exceedingly determined to earn his approval, to the extent that I would unabashedly beseech him to express his fondness towards me. What man in a sound state of judgment would reveal his profound affection for a woman after just two encounters? Indeed, you have comprehended correctly, those who have a desire to engage in sexual relations with you. That is precisely the trajectory that a considerable number of my relationships would follow rapidly. I wrongly perceived that affection as love, and upon reflection, I should have readily recognized the evident warning signs.

When you believe you have encountered the suitable individual, refrain from driving him away through premature displays of insecurity. By persisting with a gradual approach, you will not only develop a more robust bond, but also elicit a strong desire for your companionship from him. Now that you have dispatched a text message of impartial nature, all that remains is to patiently await his response. Once he responds, kindly inquire whether it would be suitable for you to reach out to him tomorrow evening, following your work. If he informs you that it is acceptable, kindly contact him via telephone upon the completion of your work on the following day. This allows him an additional two days to contemplate your actions and endeavor to comprehend the reasoning behind your deliberate pace, assuming that you have an inclination towards him. When you contact him tomorrow, inquire if he would be interested in convening for beverages at your preferred establishment or establishment of choice. Please refrain from employing the term "date" at this juncture. That alleviates the stress for both parties involved, enabling them to unwind and fully appreciate each other's companionship. Once you have come to a mutual agreement regarding a suitable venue to convene for beverages, prepare yourself for the subsequent phase, wherein you shall have the opportunity to exhibit your sociable and enjoyable qualities to him.

10. Initiate critical discussions promptly.

Marriage? Kids? Traveling? Getting settled? Pets? Following the initial date, it is not necessary to immediately propose living together to your prospective partner. Nevertheless, engaging in open discussions to ascertain their stance on fundamental matters early in the relationship can assist in preventing overstepping boundaries and subsequently experiencing dissatisfaction.

11. Please enumerate the attributes you desire in your ideal companion.

Exert adequate contemplation towards your aspirations for a committed partnership. When encountering an individual displaying promise, it is advantageous to make a conscious observation of these attributes and deliberate upon them.

12. Recognize your weaknesses

Please bear in mind that you are not without imperfections. Your kindred spirit will demonstrate a deep appreciation for your imperfections, while simultaneously urging you to further refine your character.

13. Exert effort Apply oneself diligently Commit to the task Engage in diligent labor Devote oneself to the endeavor

It is highly unlikely that your soulmate will abruptly manifest in your life. Therefore, it is imperative that you approach your endeavor with utmost seriousness. Venture outside and exert a genuine endeavor to locate them.

14. Direct your search towards the appropriate areas.

There are specific locations where it is more probable to encounter individuals who possess similar interests as you. Embark upon a tour of these locations, engage in a conversation, and pursue the dialogue.

15. Remain receptive to altering your perspective.

Having delineated a set of specific attributes you desire in a companion, it would be prudent to maintain this list as a guide while exhibiting occasional adaptability.

Maintain a consistent willingness to make compromises. Your perception of an ideal life partner will evolve with your personal growth and maturation. Do not adhere to a fixed mindset when seeking love based on the perceptions and ideals you held five years prior. Simply adhere to the guidance of your heart and allow yourself to move in harmony with the current.

16. Don\\\'t pass up opportunities.

Is one of your acquaintances attempting to orchestrate a blind date for you? Don\\\'t disregard the idea. Do not miss out on opportunities for social interaction, whether it pertains to establishing new relationships or engaging with a collective of acquaintances.

To acquire knowledge about locating your soul mate, it is recommended to maintain vigilance. Affection is a unique phenomenon that defies expectations and appears entirely out of the blue. Discovering your compatible life partner is a remarkable and invigorating experience due to this fact.

17. Apprehend the indicators that suggest something is amiss.

If one is genuinely committed to discovering their true life partner, it is imperative to discontinue any detrimental relationships. The fervor and exhilaration experienced in the early stages of a newfound love can readily obfuscate one's perception. Conversely, endeavor to discern the indicators that suggest a situation may be deceptive, thereby ensuring the efficient utilization of your time.

18. Consider chemistry.

Chemistry and passion are indispensable in any meaningful relationship, particularly when endeavoring to discover one's true soul mate. Do you maintain a positive rapport with this individual?

Exercise vigilance regarding the connection you forge as you navigate the realm of dating in pursuit of the ideal individual to designate as your soulmate. One may encounter an exceptional gentleman or an ideal lady, but oftentimes, love exhibits inexplicable characteristics.

Despite the potential for connecting two outstanding individuals, there exists the possibility that their mutual sentiment towards each other may be lacking. Within a relationship, it is essential to seek and cultivate a mutual chemistry and attraction. Do you find contentment in your current romantic relationship?

If your romantic partner doesn't generate a sense of electrical stimulation as they caress your back or fail to induce a pleasing sense of vulnerability following a first kiss, it is plausible that you could be depriving yourself of the vital phenomenon known as chemistry, a fundamental element shared by soulmates.

19. If the experience fails to evoke a lightning strike of emotion, perseverance should not be abandoned.

Exercise caution when setting expectations within your interpersonal connections. One may experience disappointment when anticipating occurrences of lightning strikes, perfection, and an impeccable connection. Ultimately, your associate will be an individual.

20. Take into consideration the factors that contribute to your compatibility.

It is imperative to bear in mind that the importance of compatibility cannot be underestimated when acquiring the ability to identify one's soulmate.

Deliberate upon the elements of your compatibility. Does it suffice?

21. Identify the key attributes of a prosperous collaboration.

Whether or not you have found your soulmate, relationships require effort. Hence, it is imperative to dedicate effort towards improving your own.

22. Exercise caution and attentiveness in your interpersonal dynamics within relationships.

It\\\'s important to communicate. If you have encountered your ideal life partner, effective communication and a mutual understanding should frequently be experienced.

23. Rapidly acquaint oneself with someone

Pose numerous inquiries and strive to develop a comprehensive understanding of an individual at the inception of a romantic relationship. One can determine if someone is their soul mate by the early acquaintance with them.

24. Strive to begin with an impartial demeanor.

Adopting a perspective that is more objective and distanced from your relationship or this individual could prove beneficial on occasions. Do not allow the allure of a new relationship to obscure your perception of the essential factors that are crucial for its success.

25. Seek advice from your acquaintances and relatives.

Your family and friends possess exceptional discernment in identifying your requirements and inclinations. Do not hesitate to inquire about their perspectives and suggestions.

26. Expand your social network.

Engaging in habitual socializing with a fixed group of individuals could pose challenges in unearthing a true soulmate. Strive to broaden your social connections and acquaint yourself with fresh faces.

1. COMMENCE COMMENDING THE RELEVANT INDIVIDUAL.

In my perspective, God is the ultimate arbiter of love narratives. By seeking His guidance, we can circumvent the perils of entangling ourselves with incompatible individuals in our romantic journeys. Consequently, soliciting divine wisdom in this context holds significant promise.

2. MAXIMIZE YOUR CAPABILITIES TO FIND YOUR LIFE PARTNER.

Do you possess an absolute certainty in your choice of being associated with the most exceptional individual? Due to the subjective nature of the term 'best,' its interpretation may vary among individuals. It remains crucial to tirelessly search and ascertain the individual most capable of fulfilling your specific needs and requirements.

That would, undoubtedly, constitute inequity should you anticipate your genuine love to possess qualities that are ideal for you while exerting no effort to exhibit those qualities in return.

Henceforth, endeavor to cultivate your utmost potential. Strive to transcend your limitations and attain your aspirations. This will facilitate an easier and more discerning assessment of compatibility between yourself and a prospective partner.

3. MAKE YOUR APPEARANCE APPEALING.

It is necessary to acknowledge the following: initial attraction precedes the experience of romantic love. Consequently, enhancing one's appearance can facilitate the identification of one's genuine love. The initial step involves presenting oneself as clean and exuding a pleasant fragrance. Thereafter, bringing attention to one's most favorable attributes or qualities is advised. Rather than concealing imperfections, one should instead devise inventive methods to enhance or, at the very least, embrace them.

CHAPTER 2

4. Determine the precise qualities and attributes you require in a prospective partner.

You may enhance your ability to discern an appropriate life partner by compiling a comprehensive list of the attributes you desire in your ideal companion. It is important to acknowledge that locating an individual embodying all these qualities in their entirety may prove challenging, as perfection is an elusive trait.

One advantage of establishing standards is that it facilitates the gathering of insights derived from past experiences with previous partners. This allows for the recollection of unfavorable attributes that were incongruous with one's own, ultimately resulting in relationship dissolution. Those who lack prior relationship experiences can draw upon interactions with individuals of the opposite sex.

5. EXPAND YOUR SOCIAL CIRCLE BY EXPANDING YOUR NETWORK OF

ACQUAINTANCES AND CULTIVATING FRIENDSHIPS.

By regularly engaging with new individuals, your likelihood of encountering your ideal romantic partner is heightened. In order to embrace a more sociable lifestyle, it is imperative to foster an outgoing demeanor. Attend social gatherings arranged by your professional network or affiliated groups. Additionally, make a conscious effort to spend time with your friends as frequently as possible. Moreover, consider becoming a member of various organizations and clubs.

6. ENGAGE IN THE APPROPRIATE ENTERPRISE." "6. PARTICIPATE IN THE SUITABLE COMPANY." "6. JOIN THE CORRECT VENTURE." "6. ALIGN WITH THE PROPER ORGANIZATION.

To increase the likelihood of encountering an ideal individual, it is advisable to position yourself in appropriate settings and surround yourself with individuals who align with your values. Consequently, exercise caution when selecting your social circle, as the individuals with whom one associates are significantly influenced by their environment.

For example, if you prefer your partner to refrain from indulging in frequent social engagements, it would be advisable to limit your interactions with friends who frequently engage in such activities. It is worth considering the adage that likeminded individuals tend to associate with one another.

Dating websites

I acknowledge that this approach may appear overly simplistic on dating platforms, however, I kindly request your patience and understanding. Despite the persistent negative perception, an increasing number of women are entering into marriage with the assistance of online dating platforms such as OKCupid, HowAboutWe, and Match, among others. Despite potential cautions about "creepers" online, I can guarantee that the atmosphere in bars can be equally questionable, and the majority of individuals seeking relationships online are willing to engage in courtship before pursuing a physical relationship.

It is imperative to maintain a receptive mindset, refraining from dismissing individuals solely based on initial encounters. Genuine contentment manifests itself once one establishes a connection with another individual, rendering the act of introductions devoid of significance if there is already an established bond.

Strategies for enticing a compatible life partner.

If one is desirous of drawing their soulmate towards them, there are several actions that can be undertaken.

Please refrain from allowing excessive levels of stress to affect you during the course of this procedure. If you possess a receptive mindset and maintain an optimistic attitude, it is likely to be effective for you.

1. Make up your mind.

The initial stage in captivating a potential romantic partner involves determining your genuine desires. When an individual's destined companion reveals themselves in their life's journey, one must possess the capacity to discern their true nature.

This is less probable if you possess uncertainty regarding your desires in a partner or within a romantic relationship. Please allocate as much time as necessary to successfully finish this phase.

2. Envision your perfect companion.

It is advisable to engage in the practice of visualizing your ideal partner in order to enhance your ability to attract a compatible soulmate. Once more, it is imperative that you acknowledge the presence of this relationship before you. Take into account the potential impact they could have on you and deliberate on how you would interact with them.

3. be thankful right now.

An additional approach to draw your significant other into your life entails cultivating a sense of gratitude for their presence in your life. If you have already expressed gratitude to the universe for bestowing upon you the love of your life, you may be astounded by the expeditious manner in which they will manifest in your existence.

Moreover, expressing gratitude could aid in preserving a positive state of mind, which could prove advantageous throughout this endeavor.

4. Acknowledge yourself

In order to draw your ideal life partner towards you, it is imperative that you develop the capacity to embrace and acknowledge your own being. If there exist facets of one's character that are displeasing, one should endeavor to rectify them or embrace them and move forward.

Undeniably, finding love can prove to be a formidable challenge if one lacks self-love.

5. Maintain confidence in your abilities

In order to attract a soulmate through the principle of the law of attraction, it is imperative to foster a profound sense of self-trust. It is imperative that you demonstrate unwavering belief in your abilities to exercise sound judgment and refrain from engaging in excessive rumination.

If you tend to be self-critical, take into account the remarkable choices you have made throughout your life.

6. Refrain from engaging in comparisons with others.

Do not engage in making comparisons with others. If an acquaintance were to encounter their soulmate during their youth, it does not necessarily preclude the possibility of discovering one's own soulmate later in life.

You may consider seeking guidance from individuals who have successfully found their soulmate in order to learn effective strategies for attracting your own compatible life partner. They might offer you some recommendations that could prove beneficial in your endeavor to find a compatible life partner.

PART TWO
SELF-HEALING TIME

LIMITING BELIEFS

Either the age exceeds or falls below my preferences."

I have made the decision to remain solitary for the remainder of my life.

I will never encounter a significant other who brings me genuine happiness.

That is an endeavor I will perpetually lack the capability to accomplish.

These phrases articulate expressions of constraining beliefs. They possess inadequate capabilities, and the presence of limiting beliefs serves as a rationalization for failing to attain one's objectives.

Constraining convictions confine us within our accustomed environments. They possess the capacity to stifle our individual and occupational advancement and achievement. These cognizant or unconscious cognitions are hypothesized to be indisputable verities.

Conversely, adverse thoughts can be conquered and substituted with more affirmative affirmations that hinder our advancement towards our life aspirations. Should you have a change of heart, it would bring about a complete transformation.

What is the reason behind our propensity for embracing such constricting beliefs?

The overwhelming majority of constraining convictions are subconsciously held convictions that materialize as a defensive mechanism in response to potential frustrations, failures, and letdowns.

It is possible that you have encountered a particular experience in the past, and currently, when confronted with a comparable circumstance, your subconscious endeavors to inhibit it. The commencement of addressing limiting beliefs can be initiated by pinpointing the root cause of such negative thoughts through identification of the influential factor.

There are several factors that can contribute to the formation of these constraining thoughts and beliefs, such as:

• Individual convictions are the result of personal encounters that have cultivated specific barriers.
We are recipients of our accumulated experiences and beliefs concerning the manner in which we were brought into existence, as well as the notions and

behaviors we witness and validate over the course of our lives.
• Fear, otherwise referred to as a pretext, pertains to any rationale one employs to evade action or engagement out of apprehension towards potential failure.

• The social circles of individuals located in your close proximity and those individuals who hold authoritative positions over you.

• Standards enforced by society can give rise to beliefs that are restrictive. • Societal norms can result in the development of limiting beliefs. • The imposition of social standards can foster the adoption of constraining beliefs. • Beliefs that constrain individuals can be imparted by societal expectations.

The dissemination of religious doctrines can occasionally propagate restrictive beliefs, as the messages conveyed by these teachings often establish norms and behaviors deemed acceptable by the deity in which an individual has faith.

To ascertain your constraining convictions, examine the objectives you aspire to achieve, yet have not yet commenced pursuing. Subsequently, examine the underlying factor that is impeding your progress in accomplishing the designated assignment. This rationale is commonly located within the "why" clause of the sentence. Attempting to unravel such constraining convictions proves to be more challenging in practice than it appears in theory.

In this scenario, engaging in meaningful conversations with individuals whom we trust, including close friends, family members, or respected mentors, can prove highly advantageous.

How, then, do you surmount your self-imposed limitations?

Recognize one of your constraining beliefs:

The initial measure in transcending your restricted convictions is to acknowledge and embrace them. If you harbor concerns regarding multiple constraints, commence by addressing the most critical one and gradually move towards the less pressing ones.

Acknowledge that it is merely a conviction.
Acknowledge that your convictions might derive from erroneous presumptions. It is highly improbable and represents a mere conjecture rather than an established truth.

Conduct a thorough evaluation of your own beliefs:
Now that you have come to the realization that it is a belief rather than a fact, it would be advisable to interrogate it. Please seek clarification by posing the question, "Is there substantial evidence supporting this belief?" Moreover, kindly provide the basis for your assertion.

Have I consistently held this perspective?

What, if any alterations, have occured? Is there any empirical evidence that would challenge or undermine my held view?

How might one's perspective be influenced by contemplating the contrasting viewpoints to their own deeply held convictions?

Is this conviction aiding me in attaining my goals?

How might one's perspective on this belief differ if viewed through the lens of individuals such as Albert Einstein, Oprah Winfrey, Steve Jobs, a business owner, a doctor, or other esteemed figures?

Several of these inquiries may initially seem peculiar, yet their purpose is to expand your comprehension of the topic. It enhances your capacity for unconventional thinking. Engaging in self-argumentation can lead you to recognize any discrepancies between your initial thoughts and your true intentions, ultimately empowering you to adopt a more constructive and motivating mindset.

Take into consideration the adverse repercussions.
What are the potential consequences of maintaining your restrictive conviction? The persistent conviction that one is incapable of succeeding in a selection process due to a prior failure can hinder their prospects of achieving success and impede their ability to lead a more prosperous life in the future.

Form a new belief:
Select a fresh set of convictions that will aid you in enhancing the quality of your life. This transition poses potential challenges. The belief may have been profoundly ingrained and emotionally intertwined, stemming from a prolonged period of contemplation and personal experience. In order to effect change, it is imperative that you possess the

fortitude and bravery to alter your mindset and embrace the new ideology.

Put it into action:

Commence taking proactive measures and establishing necessary arrangements to reinforce your newly embraced conviction. Should you hold the belief that you are "too old to commence exercising," consider embracing the belief that "it is never too late to embark on such endeavors." Proceed by undertaking a 15-minute walk today as a means to initiate exercise and establish a routine from this point onward.

Engaging in the process of conditioning oneself to adopt new beliefs encompasses the act of envisioning and mentally experiencing the desired reality for oneself. Visual representation is a superb technique for heightening anticipation. You shall possess a cognitive representation of the intended result. Consequently, your brain will transmit coherent signals, thereby facilitating its optimal function on your behalf.

To what extent does mentoring play a crucial role in the process of conquering restrictive cognitive patterns?

In conjunction with the aforementioned measures, the utilization of mentoring and coaching can yield substantial advantages in the identification and resolution of constraining convictions.
This approach utilizes a multitude of strategies in the quest for individual growth. The process of self-discovery, motivation, and drawing inspiration from accomplished individuals all constitute integral components of the mentoring journey in coaching.

Upon the realization that altering your beliefs has the potential to transform your life, you will come to the understanding that such a shift allows for the eradication of detrimental thoughts that had previously hindered your progress towards attaining your objectives. If a coach or mentor directs their attention towards your skills and their potential for enhancement, you will be motivated to surpass any self-imposed restrictions and attain your objectives.

Envision, perceive audibly, and experience the desired outcome within your consciousness. Engage in this physical activity for a minimum duration of five minutes on a daily basis. In your personal journey, you will undoubtedly witness the myriad advantages derived from engaging in this uncomplicated physical activity.

MUTUAL ACCOMMODATION: ELEMENTS THAT REQUIRE SACRIFICE TO FOSTER A FUNCTIONING RELATIONSHIP

Finding a compatible life partner poses considerable challenges. Maintaining a successful relationship requires great dedication and effort. However, for the purpose of cultivating a prosperous and lasting relationship, it is imperative to make certain concessions in order to maintain harmony. Presented herein are several items that the majority of individuals seldom relinquish.

1. Finances - Finances play a crucial role in a partnership, contributing significantly to the dynamics within. It serves as a means of collective purchase, as a method of savings for a prosperous future, and as a means of equipping one's abode. To ensure the exclusion of monetary concerns from a relationship, it is imperative to be willing to curtail one's lifestyle.

2. Interpersonal relationships - In order to cultivate a thriving alliance, one must show a willingness to relinquish certain friendships. This involves pardoning those acquaintances who fail to comprehend the dynamic of your relationship, and relinquishing associations with friends who exert a detrimental influence on your relationship.

3. Devotion - The strength of a relationship lies in the devotion you demonstrate towards it. You must be

prepared to demonstrate a steadfast commitment to your partner in order to foster a successful and enduring relationship.

4. Societal Expectations - When individuals are devoted to a partnership, a set of norms and conventions tends to emerge. Attentively heed your partner's perspectives, cater to their emotional requirements during times of distress, and refrain from ostentatiously displaying your relationship to others.

5. Relationship Norms - To foster a flourishing relationship, it is imperative to grasp the established conventions governing relationships at large. Please acknowledge that relationships seldom attain perfection and necessitate compromise to maintain harmony.

6. Personal Development - Relationships, similar to all phenomena, follow a cyclic nature. When an individual within a partnership is experiencing personal growth, it is necessary for their counterpart to demonstrate a proactive willingness to also expand and develop.

7. Intimate relations - Being in a relationship does not necessarily imply engaging in sexual activity on a daily or constant basis. It is necessary to demonstrate occasional readiness to forgo quality time with your partner in order to engage in sexual activity. It may be necessary for you to be prepared to abstain from engaging in sexual activity in order to maintain your partner's satisfaction.

8. Effective Interpersonal Communication - Effective interpersonal communication plays a pivotal role in fostering a thriving relationship, and its importance persists even after entering into a committed partnership. It is highly recommended to maintain regular communication with your partner.

9. Matrimonial Harmony - A successful partnership requires endurance, rather than haste. Your relationship will only reach its full potential when you spend a substantial duration of time together.

10. The Significance of Enjoyment - Engaging in a relationship should not preclude the pursuit of enjoyment. The

inclusion of friends and family within the dynamics of a relationship can indeed imbue it with an enjoyable quality.

11. The Significance of Objectives - A relationship entails a prolonged commitment. It is imperative to establish a goal for your relationship and demonstrate unwavering commitment towards it.

Stop waiting; start becoming!

Following the end of the relationship, I wiped away my tears and lifted myself from sorrow. I subsequently chose to relinquish my anticipation of encountering the ideal partner, as this mindset caused me distress and compelled me to endure undesirable behaviour from individuals I had encountered in the past. I established my criteria (fortunately, the breakup served as a catalyst for realigning my relationship with God and self).

I mentioned myself right? Indeed, I will be the one focusing on my own aspirations. Upon the arrival of your ideal partner, how do you envision occupying yourself? I made a conscious decision to cultivate my worth, with the hope that when we eventually crossed paths, he would regard me as a person deserving of his admiration and desire to marry. As fate would have it, my endeavor bore fruition.

Cease your passivity and idleness: while it is commendable that you possess a set of expectations regarding the attributes you desire in him, it is equally important that you take proactive measures to better yourself in anticipation of his arrival. Are you interested in a candidate from a working class background? Then embrace the role of a member of the working class. You seek a man of high virtue; to what extent do you embody such virtues as well? Are you expected to possess intellectual acumen and an exceptional level of intelligence, similar to him? Lastly, it is imperative that he possess attractive physical features, including well-groomed hands that exhibit signs of affluence. Do you meet these criteria?

Do you not aspire to avoid being a burden or leech on others? Commence the process of embodying the traits and qualities you desire to witness in others, as it is through this transformation that you shall draw individuals who align with the person you have become.

Do not possess aesthetic appeal without intellectual prowess, or possess physical form without substance. Should you desire a gentleman characterized by intellectual acumen and a scholarly nature, yet hold an aversion towards literature, a predicament will inevitably arise. Consequently, he will be deprived of engaging in intellectually stimulating discussions with you, unable to freely articulate his aspirations and anticipate your support, as you would lack the necessary understanding. This may potentially evoke feelings of inferiority as, intellectually, he possesses a greater abundance of knowledge. Therefore, commence cultivating an affinity for reading at present. Engage in the reading of literature that aligns with your specific objectives, such as works focused on matrimonial unions, along with various other subject matters.

You seek a partner from the working class, presumably due to the desire for someone capable of attending to your well-being and requirements. However, it is worth considering what contributions you will offer in return. your body? He has the ability to acquire that from any location, should he desire. What sets you apart from the others? That perspective is incorrect and displays a lack of effort, therefore it should be eliminated.

Additionally, there exists a multitude of rationales as to why one should abstain from participating in sexual activity prior to marriage.

It would be advisable for you to also commence your own efforts, as he may not be engaged in a remunerative occupation; however, if he has discerned his mission and has initiated its pursuit, that is indeed commendable. It is highly recommended that you pursue a similar approach, whereby you acquire a high-income skill in addition to your foundational academic qualifications, such as a bachelor's or master's degree.

It could encompass areas such as cake making, fashion design, software development, or any other notable skill. Currently, we are facing challenging circumstances both in Nigeria and globally, leading to widespread unemployment. However, such situations are prone to occur periodically. Nonetheless, possessing a highly profitable skill ensures that individuals have a safeguard to rely on during these trying times. It is imperative that you ascertain your purpose and commence pursuing it prior to his arrival. This will be a contributing factor in shaping his perception of you as a woman characterized by virtue.

Commence generating your own income and become a valuable asset to him upon his arrival.

Participate in seminars, conferences, and mentorship programs that align with your overarching goals and objectives. It is possible that he will come across you at one of these locations, as individuals with common interests often socialize in comparable environments.

You desire a virtuous gentleman who will offer you affection and admiration, indeed! I too aspired to such a companion! It would also benefit you to cultivate those qualities within yourself. The concept of "like begets like" is a well-known principle. Do you hold a deep reverence for God and possess an unwavering love for humanity, as the belief in the divine serves as the foundation for acquiring wisdom? Are you selfless? If you do not possess all of these qualities, it is imperative that you commence the process of cultivating them without delay. You may initiate the process by dedicating your life to Christ and extending an invitation for him to enter your life, as it is imperative to have a divine presence within you in order to embody righteousness.

Are you seeking a gentleman who embodies respect? May I inquire about your criteria for measuring respect? In the absence of monetary wealth, fame, or other material possessions, would you still hold reverence for the individual? Have you encountered instances where spouses engage in persistent criticism and disputes with their partners due to the inability to meet financial obligations? That's pathetic. If one tends to speak in a manner reminiscent of a flowing faucet, it is possible for them to engage in abusive and derogatory behavior towards individuals across various contexts. This may manifest difficulty in exhibiting proper respect towards one's spouse, particularly during moments of emotional upheaval. Initiate the practice of fostering respect by attentively minding your manner of communication, particularly when interacting with individuals of the male gender, regardless of age. Every individual, regardless of their age, wishes to avoid being treated with disrespect. In a more positive vein, I would like to mention that one of my sons is currently three years old and he anticipates your presence with great enthusiasm.

Politely express your gratitude by addressing him as 'sir' for any favors rendered, as he will persistently seek acknowledgement until you comply. To what extent is an older individual affected?

How courteous are you? As a Yoruba woman, I pride myself on our inherent courtesy, which is widely acknowledged amongst other tribes. We possess the ability to express greetings during different times of the day, such as morning, afternoon, and evening. In fact, we even have specific greetings tailored to various activities."

Eating- e wa jeun

Resting - I am in need of slumber

Taking a leisurely stroll through serene surroundings, one comes across various distractions and sights worthy of appreciation.

You are unable to deprive us of that, as it is within your capacity to adopt the practice; extend cordial greetings to individuals regardless of whether you are of Yoruba descent.

Furthermore, in regards to the topic of respect, it is important to note that when you encounter your ideal life partner, who happens to belong to the Yoruba culture, one effective approach to earn the goodwill of your prospective extended family would be to graciously adopt the custom of kneeling to greet them, accompanied by a warm and affable demeanor. I have just revealed one of my personal secrets to you, specifically pertaining to your Mother and Father-in-law.

Develop the ability to manage your emotional outbursts in public settings, considering the possibility that someone significant could potentially observe your behavior. It is conceivable that this individual may appreciate your physical appearance (the container), however, it is crucial to contemplate what lies beneath the surface (the content).

Prior to encountering my spouse, I had the opportunity to acquaint myself with his parents in advance; moreover, I used to frequent the same place of worship as them. I possessed a commendable character, as attested by others; my unique qualities were so profound that individuals were moved to tears upon my imminent departure. Due to my respectful demeanor towards the elders and children, I gained their affection. Consequently, when my ideal partner introduced me to his parents, they were delighted as they recognized that their son had made an apt selection. Transform yourself into the embodiment of your envisioned traits in your ideal life partner.

Additionally, your culinary prowess contributes significantly to your embodiment of virtuous femininity. While cooking is not exclusively associated with women, it is important to acknowledge that men should also engage in cooking. In fact, it is commendable for men to demonstrate their culinary skills as it reflects strength and authenticity. Jesus also participated in the culinary arts. However, possessing the skill and knowledge of cooking, frying, and baking can be viewed as a valuable asset on one's marital resume. etc. This also proved beneficial to me. Upon the initial visit of my significant other, he expressed great admiration for the cuisine and continues to relish in delectable meals to this day. However, it must be whispered that he possesses no fondness for the culinary arts. My husband rarely frequents fast food establishments due to his awareness that it may adversely impact his well-being.

The quality of food I prepare is inferior when compared to the meals he consumes at home, but only when he desires me to take a break. If you lack proficiency in culinary arts, now would be an opportune period to enroll in a culinary school. Acquire knowledge and enhance your skills as it is commonly believed that "the key to a person's affection lies in their stomach." In the event you wed an individual akin to my spouse who prefers not dining outside, potential disagreements may arise. Hope you understand?

13. What are the fundamental principles that dictate your actions and beliefs?

In regards to cultivating connections, which fundamental values hold significant importance for you? According to Lenhardt, it is crucial to understand and embody your core beliefs in order to achieve true happiness and success. One should not expect perfection from their partner (or vice versa), but one can hold onto the qualities they find significant in another person.

Please take the opportunity to engage in introspection, and sincerely acquaint yourself with your own identity prior to entering into a romantic partnership. What are your objectives? Your issues? Your basic beliefs? In the event that you are aware of these things, I assure you that it will lead to a more favorable situation for both you and your ideal partner.

Engaging in social interactions and having companions

Associations significantly contribute to the enhancement of one's overall well-being and prosperity.

Experiencing feelings of desolation or isolation can have an impact on your mental, personal, and physical welfare.

Individuals of greater experience who maintain strong social connections and affiliations are likely to experience an enhanced quality of life.

On this page

The field of medicine exhibits considerable strengths in terms of its numerous benefits.

The impact of desolation on one's overall welfare

Comprehensive guidelines to enhance your social connections

Sequential guidelines for establishing acquaintances with strangers.

Interconnections play a vital role in fostering social cohesion and progress within society.

Where to find support

Medical advantages are significant areas of expertise for

Throughout your lifetime, the quantity and resilience of your social relationships profoundly impact both your mental and physical well-being.

There are numerous benefits to social connections and strong mental well-being. Demonstrated alliances encompass reduced levels of anxiety and depression, heightened levels of self-assurance, enhanced empathy, and stronger bonds characterized by trust and comfort. Strong and reliable connections can also contribute to enhancing your immune system, aiding in your recovery from illnesses, and potentially prolonging your lifespan.

Fortunately, despite a considerable array of these benefits that can enhance your happiness and contentment, there is also an inherent ripple effect wherein individuals in your vicinity will seek to spend time in your company. In a similar vein, the interconnectedness of individuals leads to a virtuous cycle of societal, individual, and physical well-being.

The impact of solitude on overall mental and physical health

The condition of depression can lead to adverse emotional consequences that impact one's overall state of well-being. Depression can cause disturbances in sleep patterns, elevated blood pressure, and increased cortisol levels (a stress hormone). It has the potential to impact your immune system and diminish your overall sense of well-being. Depression is also a contributing factor to withdrawn behavior, melancholy, and suicidal tendencies.

Individuals of higher standing exhibit a particular vulnerability. In the event of a reduction in your versatility, fostering positive relationships with others can become more challenging. However, individuals of advanced age who maintain social connections and cultivate strong relationships are likely to:

experience a heightened sense of personal fulfillment

find greater contentment in their life

exhibit a reduced risk of developing dementia and experiencing cognitive decline

need less homegrown help.

The demographic comprising younger individuals, namely adolescents and those in their 20s, are equally susceptible to being adversely affected when they experience social isolation. Lack of social connections can directly impact a child's physical well-being by elevating the risk of obesity, inflammation, and high blood pressure.

These three medical conditions have the potential to give rise to chronic medical complications, such as cardiovascular disease, cerebrovascular accident, and malignancies. However, a diverse social network can serve as a protective factor against physical deterioration.

Furthermore, the benefits of social connections are essential, irrespective of the mitigation of other factors contributing to mortality such as socioeconomic status, tobacco and alcohol consumption, obesity, and unemployment. In conclusion, irrespective of leading a healthy lifestyle, it is imperative to maintain a robust social engagement to ensure wellness and happiness.

It is imperative to discern that desolation is distinct from solitude. Experiencing a sense of desolation poses a concern; however, being isolated from others may not be a concern at all. Numerous individuals reside in solitude and experience profoundly contented and fulfilling existences.

Guidelines for enhancing your interpersonal connections

Attempting to acclimate oneself to a state of desolation can be a formidable challenge. Fortunately, there are steps you can take to effectively manage and cope with depression. As an illustration, one can foster enduring relationships with individuals who provide support by dedicating time to their companionship, and by striving to engage in regular conversations with them.

There exist three types of affiliations that can be established with individuals:

personal relationships - with individuals who harbor affection and concern for you, such as esteemed acquaintances interpersonal affiliations - involving individuals whom you regularly encounter and have a common interest, such as colleagues or the individuals who prepare your daily coffee

Unify affiliations - involving individuals who have a common group membership or a connection with you, such as those who align with your voting preferences or individuals who share a similar belief system.

Pose this question to yourself: do you possess substantial, enduring alliances within this considerable multitude of three respective regions?

Perhaps you tend to maintain enduring relationships with lifelong companions and do not currently feel prepared to acquaint yourself with unfamiliar individuals. Alternatively, you may choose to avoid individuals from your past, instead preferring to associate with people who have limited or no knowledge of your personal history. Adopt a candid approach when assessing your social inclinations.

Reflect upon the relationships you currently share with individuals, as well as the relationships you may aspire to establish. It may be necessary for you to establish new affiliations, or alternatively, you may consider endeavors to fortify your existing associations.

One strategy for enhancing your social networks involves establishing connections with familiar individuals in your life, such as colleagues, family members, classmates, or neighbors. Kindly initiate communication with an individual of your choice, whether by making a phone call or by drafting and sending an email, to convey your interest in maintaining more frequent contact with them. Arrange to partake in an espresso or a banquet, or to linger while listening to music, engage in a round of golf, or indulge in a game of chess. Reflect upon the mutual interests you possess. Facebook and other virtual entertainment platforms serve as excellent means of maintaining communication.

Avoiding competition.

On certain occasions, the act of observing adoration entails a sense of vulnerability and taking risks. This can be particularly disconcerting when we realize that we will be required to participate in a specific level of competition. It is not imperative that we adopt a competitive approach to dating or engage in adversarial behavior, but we must acknowledge that we may encounter competitive attitudes, both within ourselves and from others. According to Dr. Firestone's assertion, "Our apprehension towards competition may compel us to avoid drawing attention to ourselves." We may have concerns about appearing foolish or being overlooked. We may harbor apprehensions regarding triumphing over the opposition, as we may fear causing offense to others. Striving for our desires can evoke fear, but acknowledging the competitive sentiments that arise can help us avoid self-deprecation or unfairly critiquing others, instead of honestly acknowledging our desires and maintaining a determined mindset. If we choose to refrain from participating (such as choosing to remain at home instead of attending a gathering, withholding self-assurance in introductions, or avoiding conversation) due to our discomfort with these emotions, we may deprive ourselves of a fulfilling experience.

Maintaining Our Established Sphere of Familiarity

A significant multitude of individuals establish mental frameworks defining their identity and capabilities, actively adhering to these constructs throughout their lifetimes. We manufacture partitions designed to safeguard our emotions. We are dissatisfied with the fact that we do not venture out or experience uneasiness when encountering new individuals. Nonetheless, we refrain from confronting such circumstances due to our desire to remain within our comfort zone. For certain individuals, this may entail seeking detachment. For individuals, this may involve exerting genuine effort and demonstrating competence. Many people are willing to engage in introspection, even when their inner thoughts might be harsh or negative, as they prioritize being authentic and attuned to their own instincts. Understanding the purpose and functionality of this air pocket can enable us to commence our efforts to disrupt the closed paradigm that limits our choices.

That Thing Called Confidence

An ideal woman does not meet everyone's expectations. She is primarily focused on fulfilling her own desires. That signifies her possession of self-assurance and poise. Curiously, confidence does not stem from the absence of fear or complete emotional control. Furthermore, it does not entail concealing one's insecurities and vulnerabilities.

Upon initially acquiring knowledge about confidence and grasping its concepts, I became cognizant of its significance as a powerful tool for personal advancement, perceiving it as a valuable key to unlock one's potential. It's so counterintuitive.

If individuals were educated in the academic setting about the universal presence of insecurities and vulnerabilities among all people. If only we had realized that demonstrating normalcy was expected. We could have alleviated ourselves from a considerable amount of anguish and distress.

As such, it is important to bear in mind that each of us harbors feelings of anxiety and insecurity. The sole disparity lies in the fact that individuals exhibiting significant confidence have consciously or subconsciously grasped this principle and are willing to openly disclose what those lacking confidence are apprehensive about revealing.

Individuals who lack confidence believe that divulging their insecurities will result in being perceived as feeble or lacking value, yet the contrary holds true. Individuals possess the ability to discern our genuine disclosure of vulnerabilities and apprehensions. The greater our efforts to conceal these emotions, the more prominently they manifest.

Now, there is no need for you to vocalize your insecurities and vulnerabilities for the entire world to hear. It is important to bear in mind that one should not hesitate to acknowledge and openly embrace these aspects. The focus does not lie in assuming a victim mentality or seeking attention based on personal insecurities; rather, it entails demonstrating a genuine embrace of one's human experience through acceptance, courage, and compassion. You will exude an air of self-assurance by adhering to these guidelines.

The Focus is Evidenced in One's Attitude

An ideal embodiment of femininity does not embody thoughtlessness. That does not possess an appealing quality, instead, it reveals a higher level of bitterness and apprehension rather than any other characteristic. Demonstrating compassion toward others reflects a truly virtuous character. Exhibit kindness, display respect, demonstrate curiosity, embody integrity, and showcase authenticity, for these qualities epitomize genuine beauty.

Do not insult anybody. Exercise restraint in passing judgment on any matter. Do not harbor feelings of jealousy or engage in the act of comparing oneself with others. Remember, you are unique.

It is not necessary for you to eradicate your past in order to cultivate a dreamlike state or find happiness. Your previous experiences have molded and influenced your present identity. That warrants recognition. This phenomenon holds particularly true in the event of experiencing defeat in certain conflicts. In this particular scenario, it is of utmost importance that one refrains from squandering the opportunity to derive valuable insights from previous missteps.

Your encounters are bound to foster profound personal growth within you.

Your attained outcomes are contingent upon the disposition you adopt. I hold the perception that there exist three primary states in which an individual can undergo transformation.

One could effectively convey the same message in a formal tone by stating: "To explicate the process of transformation comprehensively, it is most prudent to examine the metaphorical journey of the carrot, the egg, and the coffee bean, as they each endured an arduous yet profoundly transformative process." They were subjected to an equal degree of heat (pressure), however, the subsequent outcomes exhibited stark contrasts.

The carrot initially displayed robustness, yet upon thermal exposure, it underwent a transition to a tender and feeble state.

The egg initially exhibited a firm exterior and a tender interior, but subsequent to being subjected to heat, the egg's interior has solidified.

In contrast, the coffee bean exhibited distinct characteristics. He altered both the hue and the fragrance of the water.

The coffee bean emerged as the unequivocal victor of the encounter. He remained steadfast in his character despite the profoundness of the experience. He undertook the task of transforming and enhancing both his surroundings and his own being.

Certainly, your convictions regarding the ideal manner in which life should unfold and the expectations you hold regarding life's trajectory will significantly influence your process of self-transformation following a profound experience. However persuasive your convictions may be, there is no obligation to unquestioningly embrace them.

You possess the inherent ability to exercise discretion, and you can exercise your volition in determining your beliefs and cultivating your desired dispositions in life. Contemplate upon the disposition one possesses when undergoing a profoundly impactful encounter.

Consider the profound impact on your life that would ensue if you consistently adopted the mentality attributed to the coffee bean.

The focus is not on finding ways to simplify matters, but on effectively optimizing any given circumstance.

Rather than consistently seeking the path of least resistance, we ought to strive for a superior alternative.

Becoming physically fit illustrates how to navigate challenges effectively. During my fitness classes, when I observe the group struggling with a particular exercise, I often jestingly convey to them that there exists no alternative means to achieve physical fitness. I inform them that regrettably, discomfort is an inherent aspect of the process necessary to achieve the desired outcomes.

Do not allow apprehension to hinder you, as it is an inherent aspect of the progression. The outcomes justify the effort.

If you have experienced emotional distress in the past and currently find yourself unattached, desiring to pursue romantic connections again may entail a concerted effort to restore and bolster your self-assurance promptly.

In retrospect, in the distant future, your greatest regret may lie not in the actions you pursued, but rather in the opportunities you failed to seize. Throw off the bowlines. Set sail and venture beyond the confines of the familiar harbor. Harness the prevailing trade winds in your sails. Explore. Dream. Discover." [i]

In order to achieve your desires and aspirations, it is imperative to prioritize them on your agenda rather than relegating them to the realm of mere wishful thinking. Consider it as an established fact. One should possess the ability to perceive and experience it. This will all be operative within your cognition, directing your energy towards the precise objective. No obstacles impede your priorities.

I distinctly recall expressing to an acquaintance, "I possess a clear understanding of my desires and I am confident in my ability to attain them." I remain uncertain as to the method, but I am determined to resolve this matter. There was unequivocal certainty, devoid of any hesitations or reservations. This principle dictated my lifestyle, influencing all my endeavors with the sole purpose of attaining it.

This identical procedure has facilitated numerous individuals in attaining their desires, irrespective of their initial circumstances. They facilitate its realization, as it was regarded as a priority rather than a mere aspiration. The key to achieving success in any endeavor lies in determining the means to make things function effectively, rather than attempting to force them into conformity with personal expectations. In order to bring about any desired changes or improvements in your life, it is important to carefully observe how things operate and seek guidance from individuals who possess greater knowledge in the matter.

Do not let fear of failure hinder you, for in the face of adversity, seize the opportunity to gain knowledge, rise above, and make a renewed attempt. When you embrace the courage to confront your fears and demonstrate unwavering perseverance despite encountering obstacles, the inevitability of success arises. On the day that you make the choice, I will undertake all appropriate measures to restore my confidence, trust, and happiness. It will signal the commencement of a journey towards healing and triumph. Henceforth, you shall experience the sensation of vitality.

I am confident that this aligns with your aspirations and ambitions in life.

It is imperative to constantly bear in mind that an existence defined by flawlessness is unattainable. Joy is accompanied by slight unease. That's it!

The enchantment constitutes the initial component of the equation for a contented and enduring partnership, and is bestowed by your gracious presence. It is conveyed through the embodiment of your composed, joyful, optimistic, cultivated, and imaginative character.

You hold the power to shape the trajectory of your life and all of the connections you forge. When experiencing such emotions, one is truly embracing their holistic femininity. You are self-sufficient and do not require external presence to experience such emotions.

You possess the essence of enchantment in your life, whether you find yourself unattached or engaged in a partnership. This stands out as being among your most crucial assets and convictions. Place your trust in yourself and the strength of your distinctiveness, for it is this attribute that grants enduring steadiness, assurance, and affection.

If you fail to cultivate your self-assurance and prioritize personal growth, it is highly probable that you will encounter difficulties in attaining a sense of empowerment, thereby leading to a relationship that may fall short of your initial expectations.

Having a positive perspective on life cultivates self-assurance and directs one's attention towards transformative actions within their circumstances. Upon completing this task, you will acquire the resilience needed to establish essential parameters within a relationship that promote well-being and contentment.

There exists a wide array of individuals of various characteristics, however, it is primarily those individuals who are drawn to self-assured women that possess the ability to foster a substantial and gratifying relationship. Therefore, the sole means of procuring an outstanding romantic partner is by enhancing one's own personal development initially.

Step #3

This subsequent section may elicit some emotional response, as it is commonly observed that, following the conclusion of a relationship, regardless of its duration, be it a brief period or a lengthy period of matrimony, lingering emotions such as hurt, resentment, and anger are often present. In Part III, I will assist you in liberating yourself from the hindrances that have prevented you from cultivating the desired relationship. For the time being, let us examine your previous relationships from an alternate perspective.

Regardless of how tumultuous a relationship may have concluded, it is always possible to reflect upon fond memories. Instances such as the initial encounter, marked by the inception of captivating chemistry... the emergence of deep affection... the inaugural intimate experience, along with subsequent instances. Trips you took. It is highly likely that we will have accumulated a substantial collection of pleasant memories. I kindly request you to engage in the following exercise as a means to enhance your understanding and obtain clarity about your desires within your envisioned relationship.

• Compile a comprehensive inventory of favorable aspects derived from previous romantic partnerships that you aspire to experience within your future relationship. It encompasses actions performed towards and on behalf of your partner(s), reciprocated actions received from them, rewarding experiences encountered during travels, social engagements, personal emotions or sentiments, and any other thoughts that may arise. Simply proceed through your roster of interpersonal connections, recollecting the moments of joy and positivity.

Now, upon reviewing the aforementioned list that you have compiled, which items would you classify as pertaining to your distinctive interpersonal aptitudes and not his? How did you manage to cultivate such beneficial events, behaviors, and encounters within your relationships?

- Within the pages of your journal, expound upon your strengths with meticulous elaboration.

Ensuring the incorporation and utilization of those skills within your new relationship can be accomplished through what means?

- Please proceed to provide your response at this moment.

I believe it is imperative that you undertake these assignments, as they will facilitate the development of heightened self-awareness and conscientiousness regarding your actions and interpersonal responses. By increasing your level of consciousness, you will acquire a higher level of preparedness to conduct yourself in a manner aligned with your intentional choices, as opposed to acting out of unconscious instinct. It is the impulsive responses that frequently lead to adverse consequences for each and every one of us.

Prior to concluding this section, I would like to encourage each individual to allocate a moment to acknowledge the positive aspects present in each of these relationships. This will assist you in relinquishing any lingering feelings of anger, pain, animosity, or bitterness that you might be holding onto. Clinging to such pessimistic energy will not only prevent you from attracting a remarkable gentleman, but it will also induce your energy to repulse well-suited suitors.

In the event that you are unwilling to relinquish those negative emotions, it is advisable to introspect and question the underlying reasons. What benefits do you derive from retaining such detrimental energy? While it may necessitate your willingness to engage in uncomfortable sincerity, this approach has the potential to uncover significant insights.

• Should you be disinclined to recognize the positive aspects and instead choose to hold onto your feelings of hurt and anger, you may acquire valuable insights by exploring the reasons behind such emotions within the pages of your journal.

Step #4

Now that we have revisited pleasant recollections, let us diverge onto a contrasting path and explore the realm of unfavorable reminiscences. However, the focus of our discussion shall not be centered around the aforementioned topic of holding onto past grievances, anger, and resentments. This concerns adopting a more pragmatic approach rather than an emotional one.

This presents an occasion to examine prior patterns, anticipations, and the manner in which conflicts arose between the two parties. Essentially, what is termed as the "dysfunctional elements of your relationships" in popular psychology can be attributed to three factors: those that were innate to you, those that were inherited from your previous partners, and those that arose as a result of your union.

The objective of this exercise is to ascertain the factors that were ineffective in your past relationships, in order to cultivate your awareness of these aspects. If an individual lacks clarity regarding their aspirations for the future, it is highly likely that they will unintentionally carry unresolved issues into subsequent relationships.

Some examples are:

• You allow him to have full autonomy in decision-making.

• You revealed aspects of your authentic identity • You divulged fragments of your genuine self • You exposed elements of your real personality

• You monopolized all the decision-making and deprived him of any input

• You allowed him to speak with disrespect towards him

- Your manner of speaking to him was disrespectful.

- You refrained from expressing your discontent and chose to remain silently brooding rather than communicate with him.

- You became upset without facilitating a composed discussion between adults.

- You compromised on unsatisfying or infrequent sexual experiences.

- You withheld sexual intimacy from him as a form of punishment.

Compile a comprehensive inventory of negative experiences from previous relationships that you would strongly prefer to avoid in your prospective relationship. It encompasses actions directed towards your partner(s), actions received from them, modes of communication, allocation of time, personal disposition, and any other relevant reflections. Utilize the aforementioned list as a means of invoking your memory. Examine your roster of past relationships and recollect the unfavorable habits and modes of interaction that you ought not to replicate in your forthcoming relationship.

- Please document your thoughts and reflections in your personal journal.

Now, carefully analyze the list you have crafted to identify those items that are directly tied to your own distinct interpersonal skills - or, to be more precise, your deficiency in these skills - rather than attributing them to him. A few of these will merely manifest as unfavorable practices. In order for this process to be effectively beneficial, it is imperative that you maintain a high level of sincerity. This will remain confidential and is exclusively intended for your eyes only.

Did these tendencies emerge from a specific relationship, were they acquired from past relationships, or were they inherited from observing the dynamics of your family members, notably your parents?

Please proceed to provide your responses at this time.

How can one ensure that these negative habits do not permeate their newfound relationship?

Please proceed with providing your responses at this time.

You are Wonderful!

If one continually affirms their wonderful qualities, they will eventually come to believe, manifest, and embody their inherent wonderfulness.

~ Marrilyn S.H. Tong, Esq." "~ Marrilyn S.H. Tong, JD" "~ Marrilyn S.H. Tong, LL.B." "~ Marrilyn S.H. Tong, Barrister" "~ Marrilyn S.H. Tong, Solicitor

You are wonderful. Yes, YOU!

What are your sentiments upon perusing the aforementioned statement? Did you feel happy? Did you experience a sense of joy, yet perceive it as deceptive? Alternatively, did you perceive that statement as untrue and find it challenging to acknowledge?

This principle also extends to the manner in which we accept compliments. How do you respond when someone offers you a compliment? Please take into consideration that occasionally we reciprocate expressions of gratitude as a gesture of politeness, however, what is your genuine sentiment regarding this matter?

If the act of receiving compliments causes you discomfort, shame, or feelings of undeserving, it is essential for you to grasp the importance and value of compliments. They represent tokens and embodiments of affection in diverse manners. Every individual is entitled to love and acceptance, and it is imperative that each person is duly acknowledged. When we are able to acknowledge and value the affection demonstrated towards us by various individuals, both personally and professionally, we are also affirming our acceptance of a life that we have acquired the ability to deeply cherish.

The perception others have of you will reflect your self-perception and self-conduct. If one perceives oneself to be exceptional, it is likely that others will perceive one as exceptional. By consistently affirming your own beauty on a daily basis, it is conceivable that you will ultimately begin to receive commendations from others regarding your exceptional beauty. In order to attain love, it is imperative that we cultivate a deep sense of love within ourselves.

What if you harbor negative thoughts about yourself?

The majority of individuals have cultivated adverse internal self-dialogue or engage in self-assessment with critical connotations. I kindly request your participation in the endeavor to enact modifications to these statements and substitute them with affirmative assertions.

Do you frequently engage in self-comparisons with others? Do you experience profound self-acceptance and contentment with your authentic self?

A portion of individuals are delaying self-acceptance until they achieve weight loss objectives, apply cosmetics, attain desired financial gains, or establish other self-imposed prerequisites. May I inquire as to what you are currently delaying for? Do it now.

According to my sister, during her makeup application, she gazes into the mirror and affirms, "Indeed, I am exceptionally attractive!" Subsequently, when she ventures outdoors or mingles with acquaintances, she receives acknowledgments regarding her remarkable beauty. I believe that is a commendable notion and it should be adopted by all individuals as well.

The repetitive verbalization of one's thoughts has the potential to manifest them into reality. This comprises not only all the positive assertions and convictions you express regarding yourself, but also, regrettably, the negative ones. Presently, the imperative task at hand is to cultivate a heightened sense of attentiveness towards the internal dialogue that transpires within oneself on a consistent basis.

Do you refer to yourself as unintelligent when you make a minor error? Alternatively, do you believe that you are devoid of love, devoid of interesting qualities, or burdened by other unfavorable traits? In future occurrences of this nature, it is suggested that you consciously observe such behavior, acknowledge it with amusement, and proceed to replace it with a constructive affirmation concerning your own abilities.

The initial procedure for eliminating a detrimental belief that we hold about ourselves is to promptly recognize it occurring. By adopting this approach, we will be able to acknowledge and subsequently address the issue at hand. The majority of our actions, behaviors, and internal dialogues tend to operate on autopilot, akin to an unfavorable habitual pattern. For instance, in instances where an error is made, there is a propensity to label oneself as unintelligent. It is plausible that you have been engaged in this activity for such an extensive duration that you have become oblivious to your own actions.

In the future, please exercise caution regarding the automatic behaviors that you exhibit. Exercise caution and display attentiveness towards your responses to various situations. Take note of the internal dialogues that occur within your mind, as well as the manner in which you communicate with others about your emotions and all other relevant matters. Become aware of your actions, recognize them, and make efforts to modify them.

Let us embark on the journey to cultivate a renewed version of your individuality. When one develops a profound affection for oneself, invariably, the rest of the world shall be captivated by one's essence as well. I kindly request your thoughtful consideration

YOU ARE THE SOURCE.

The possibilities of creation are boundless. You inhabit a realm characterized by infinite possibilities, wherein you should always bear in mind that the attainment of anything is within your reach. It is high time that you cultivate self-love.

~ Exercise ~

Record in a personal journal or transcribe onto a sheet of paper a collection of twenty commendable attributes that pertain to your character. If it is possible for you to compose a list of up to 50 attributes, that would be even more advantageous. Please ensure this item remains in close proximity to your bedside for convenient retrieval. Delve into the depths, and you will encounter astonishing discoveries.

These qualities may extend to various aspects of one's life and should not be limited solely to interpersonal connections.

Please consult this written list whenever you find yourself engaging in self-criticism or experiencing a sense of melancholy. This exercise is intended for the cultivation of self-affection and to serve as a gentle reminder of one's inherent magnificence.

Please transcribe all the favorable character attributes you desire for yourself onto a separate page or sheet of paper. For instance, in the event that one perceives oneself to possess a diminished level of assurance, it would be beneficial to document the aspiration to experience a heightened sense of self-assurance and comport oneself accordingly.

If one is dissatisfied with their overall appearance, they should identify the aspects they wish to appreciate and cultivate a sense of positivity towards them.

I request that you compose the sentences in the present tense, to reflect the current moment. Please record solely affirmative statements, abstaining from stating any negative opinions regarding yourself.

The subconscious mind lacks a sense of humor and is unable to differentiate between actuality and a mental construct. The thoughts that consistently occupy our minds will eventually materialize in our reality. It is crucial, therefore, to exercise caution in selecting our words meticulously and concentrating solely on optimistic thoughts.

Our objective entails repeatedly reaffirming these desired traits to oneself, until such a point where one genuinely internalizes and believes them across all dimensions of their existence, thereby manifesting the desired transformation into the person they aspire to be.

Experience a sense of ownership or possession. Own them. Be them. Initially, one may perceive a sense of self-deception. Keep going. Over time, you will gradually come to possess them fully.

Embrace yourself warmly and express affection towards your own reflection by verbalizing your love every day while standing before a mirror.

Compose a personal correspondence expressing adoration towards oneself.

Over the course of the next 30 days, it is recommended that you peruse these materials each morning immediately following awakening, as well as in the evenings prior to retiring for the night. Please be mindful that you can contribute additional items to the lists at any point during this exercise. . . and watch what happens!

Please set aside this book for the time being and proceed with the subsequent section tomorrow.

www.ingramcontent.com/pod-product-compliance
Lightning Source LLC
Chambersburg PA
CBHW050245120526
44590CB00016B/2226